The Pursuit
of Excellence

The Pursuit of Excellence

Ted W. Engstrom

Executive Director
World Vision

Zondervan Publishing House
of The Zondervan Corporation
Grand Rapids, Michigan

THE PURSUIT OF EXCELLENCE
© 1982 by The Zondervan Corporation
Grand Rapids, Michigan

Library of Congress Cataloging in Publication Data

Engstrom, Theodore Wilhelm
    The pursuit of excellence.

    Includes bibliograhical references.
    1. Christian life—1960– . I. Title.
BV4501.2.E584   248.4   82-2683
Cloth: ISBN 0-310-24240-1   AACR2
Paper: ISBN 0-310-24241-X

Edited by Betsy Stine and Judith E. Markham
Designed by Ann Cherryman

Printed in the United States of America

82 83 84 85 86 87 88 / 10 9 8 7 6 5 4 3 2

*To Ed Dayton
who, more than any other,
has helped me
pursue excellence*

Contents

Foreword

No matter who you are, what you do, or where you come from, *The Pursuit of Excellence* was written specifically for you.

This book at times gently urges, and at other moments compels you to realize your potential, to look at yourself and compare the person that you could be with who you are. It accuses each of us of being eager and willing to take the easy way out, of waiting for perfection and success to come our way while living a life of mediocrity. It will humble and embarrass you as it did me when you realize that Ted Engstrom is talking about you with an accuracy that makes you wonder if he was following you through a day's activity.

After being led through the shock of self-discovery, the book inspires a determination to change destructive habits and debilitating perceptions and to begin the pursuit of excellence. Dr. Engstrom provides a well-defined and rational course of action without succumbing to a simplistic formula. It is not an easy task . . . but he argues convincingly that it is worth the effort. You will be encouraged with analysis of what you can expect on the journey. You will be inspired by the illustrations of those who have gone before.

In these challenging times, it is urgent that people of faith be all they can be after the admonition of the Apostle Paul to "earnestly desire the higher gifts. And I will show you a more excellent way" (1 Cor. 12:31). I encourage you to read, mark, and digest this excellent book and be faithful to all that you are meant to be.

MARK O. HATFIELD
U.S. Senator—Oregon

Preface

For a dozen or more years, my friend and colleague Ed Dayton and I have been conducting two-day "Managing Your Time" seminars all across America (and in many parts of the world), attended now by thousands of Christian leaders. The first day of the seminar material has been published in the book *Strategy for Living* (Regal), and the second day in *Strategy for Leadership* (Revell).

At the close of the first seminar day, I give a lecture I entitle "The Pursuit of Excellence," which seemingly has been helpful and encouraging to our seminar participants.

My friend, publisher Pat Zondervan, has heard this lecture and has encouraged me to enlarge upon it and develop this important theme more fully. Thus this book. I trust it will be an encouragement to many to live lives more fully and productively, to the glory of God.

I am most deeply indebted to my friend Bob Larson for his much-appreciated assistance, guidance, and research for this project. He fully believes in this "pursuit" and has enabled me to bring this concept, in which I so strongly believe, into print.

TED W. ENGSTROM

The Pursuit
of Excellence

Compared with what we ought to be, we are only half awake. Our fires are damped, our drafts are checked. We are making use of only a small part of our possible mental and physical resources.

William James

1

Give Up Your Small Ambitions

An American Indian tells about a brave who found an eagle's egg and put it into the nest of a prairie chicken. The eaglet hatched with the brood of chicks and grew up with them.

All his life, the changeling eagle, thinking he was a prairie chicken, did what the prairie chickens did. He scratched in the dirt for seeds and insects to eat. He clucked and cackled. And he flew in a brief thrashing of wings and flurry of feathers no more than a few feet off the ground. After all, that's how prairie chickens were supposed to fly.

Years passed. And the changeling eagle grew very old. One day, he saw a magnificent bird far above him in the cloudless sky. Hanging with graceful majesty on the powerful wind currents, it soared with scarcely a beat of its strong golden wings.

"What a beautiful bird!" said the changeling eagle to his neighbor. "What is it?"

"That's an eagle—the chief of the birds," the neighbor clucked. "But don't give it a second thought. You could never be like him."

So the changeling eagle never gave it another thought. And it died thinking it was a prairie chicken.[1]

What a tragedy. Built to soar into the heavens, but conditioned to stay earthbound, he pecked at stray seeds and chased insects. Though designed to be among the most awesome of all fowl, instead, he believed his neighbor's counsel: "Hey, you're only a prairie chicken. . . . Come on, let's go find us some insects."

Right now, you may find yourself in a situation much like that changeling eagle. You know you are designed to perform tasks far greater than you've performed to date. You know you have the ability to move well beyond your present self-imposed limitations. But for some reason, you do not choose the path of excellence. You're an eight-cylinder automobile straining on four.

You say, "After all, it's so much easier to scavenge for insects than to soar among the heavens. It's so much easier to accept the status quo than to venture out," Of course it is. It's also easier to enjoy long, nonproductive lunches and attend seminar after seminar on "how to do it" than to sit down and get the job done.

But that which is easy and nondemanding is seldom truly fulfilling. And it is 180 degrees away from the path toward personal excellence.

As we work out a strategy for pursuing excellence in these chapters, I think you'll realize that today is the today to start giving up your small ambitions. Right now, you can begin living your life with a vigor, enthusiasm, and intensity you never before imagined. Starting today, you can begin to draw from your own deep inner resources and cut a swath through mediocrity that will give your life a whole new significance. The results of your efforts may so surprise you that you'll wonder why you waited so long. You'll also find that your mind, stretched to a new idea or new action, will never retreat to its original dimension.

But a word of caution: Every truly worthwhile achievement of excellence has a price tag. The question you must answer for yourself is, How much am I willing to pay in hard work, patience, sacrifice, and endurance to be a person of excellence? Your answer is important, because the cost *is* great. But if you are willing to be the person you were meant to be, I think you will discover that *for you* the sky is the limit, because each one of us is called by God to become personally involved in an act of creation. Excellence is not restricted to sex, age, race, or occupation. This means a life of excellence is for *you.*

You may be a pastor, a student in seminary, a carpenter, an executive, a teacher. You may be a mother who every day tries to relate to two-and three-year-olds. You may be a parent of teenagers (a special prayer is said here for you). You may be young, or you may be in retirement. Whoever you are, today *is* the first day of the rest of your life—a day of new resolve and new beginnings. What will you make of these precious hours? Are you going to live the half life of a prairie chicken, scratching for seeds and insects? Or will you choose to soar, to build a personal reputation for excellence . . . to live your life as God intended, knowing that He loves you dearly and that He wants the very best for your life? I hope you'll accept the challenge to make this day a truly new day.

J.B. Phillips paraphrases Philippians 1:10 as follows: "I want you to be able always to recognize the highest and the best, and to live sincere and blameless lives until the day of Christ." In the New International Version the apostle's prayer is that we "may be able to discern what is best."

The highest and the best—this should be the goal of every man and woman of God.

Be the best person you know how to be, in your personal life and on the job.

If you're not stretching yourself and your talents, ask yourself why not? And then do something about it.

Give up your small ambitions. Believe a big God; remember that "God is greater"!

Get angry with your own mediocrity, and then do something constructive to get yourself out of the same old rut.

Don't wait for the seventh wave of success to carry you on to the comfort of the shore. That's the thinking of the irresponsible and the lazy. With God as your strength, take responsibility for your own actions and begin living life with a fresh point of view.

An exciting life of excellence awaits you—and it can begin today.

The admonition of the apostle Paul in Colossians 3:17 is to the point: "And whatever you do, in word or deed, do everything in the name of the Lord Jesus, giving thanks to God the Father through him." No greater standard for excellence can be found anywhere!

Again the apostle says in Philippians 4:8, (NIV) "If anything is excellent . . . think about such things."

But among many Christians, there are some serious tensions in the pursuit—or nonpursuit—of excellence. There are conflicts over what is highest and best. Some people feel the church should be a nickel and dime operation. Others choose to mortgage their grandchildren's future on the building of lavish cathedrals. Often, there's a curious mix.

I once visited a beautiful chapel on a new church college campus. In contrast to three obviously expensive chandeliers was a hand-drawn Sunday school attendance chart taped on the foyer wall. Twenty-five hundred dollars for chandeliers, but the best they could do to communicate what was happening to *people* was a crude graph.

A few years ago, we at World Vision were strongly criticized for purchasing first quality plumbing for a new building (a long-term investment that has paid good dividends). But at the time, to some, it seemed "too good." There's also been occasional criticism for our having carpeting in many of our offices, instead of linoleum. "It looks too posh," one said. "It doesn't look Christian," said another. (I've never quite figured out what a Christian carpet might look like!) Someone else offered, "It won't be a good witness. It looks too nice." Well, I couldn't disagree more. Somewhere in my files I have the actual yearly cost breakdown of how much World Vision has saved in linoleum wax alone. But that carpet also reduces noise and distraction, and thus helps our staff get the work done in considerably less time. As far as the Christian witness is concerned, we believe that appearance *is* important. We make no apologies for first-class appearance, because we as Christ's people are called to excellence. Further, we believe we are to *set the standards* of excellence for ourselves and others.

But "clothes don't necessarily make the person," and there is always the issue of confusing shadow with substance. Carpet on the floor will not hide shoddy work at the desk. That is why the quality of excellence must pervade our entire lives. It's so much more than just appearance. Scripture reminds us, "Let *all things* be done decently and in order."

In his book *Making It Happen*, Charles Paul Conn writes:

Whatever it is
However impossible it seems
Whatever the obstacle that lies between you and it
If it is noble
If it is consistent with God's kingdom, you must
   hunger after it and stretch yourself to reach it.

Have you ever watched a dramatic movie about mountain climbing, where the camera follows the climbers close up as they inch their way 180 degrees into the heavens, grasping and reaching for every little crevice of rock which in turn gives them a new footing to move up still a few more inches? And haven't you felt, Wow, I could never do that? You've got to be born a mountain goat to make that kind of a climb. But some of you *have* tried it, haven't you? And you've actually lived to discuss the experience. Sure, it was tough, exhausting, and frightening. But you did it. You moved beyond yourself. You gave up the comfort of the common plateau and headed toward greater heights. And you made it!

But mountains aren't the only challenges. What about your everyday life? How exciting are your sixteen waking hours each day? Are you constantly challenging yourself, straining your muscles? Or are you settling for less than the best?

If so, is it because you feel uneasy with the idea of having the best, being the best, or doing something that is truly outstanding? Do you find it easier to handle "excellence" if you can shift the responsibility for it onto someone else—or *onto the Lord*: "The Lord has really blessed his ministry," or, "The Lord really gave her great gifts"? Do you even feel somehow less spiritual if there is direct praise for a job done with *excellence*?

"To God be the glory" is more than the poetry of a song. It's the truth. God is the source of all our strength and to Him all glory and honor is due. But God has always chosen to use people like you and me. Frail? Yes. Prone to mistakes? Of course. Perfect? Never. But with all the things we can list that are wrong with us, there is still one overriding cry from the heavens: "I love you, and you are my children." When it comes to people, God never has made junk. And besides that, as Ethel Waters used to say, "He's never been guilty of sponsoring a flop."

Striving for excellence in our work, whatever it is, is not only our Christian duty, but a basic form of Christian witness. And our nonverbal communication speaks so loudly that people often cannot hear a single word we say.

Dr. David McClellan, professor of psychology at Harvard, says, "Most people in this world can be divided into *two* broad groups. There is that *minority* which is challenged by opportunity and is willing to work hard to achieve something, and the *majority*, which really does not care all that much."

Which camp are you in? Are you willing to work at being good at something? Really good? Are you willing to spend your life building a reputation? Or will you settle for the life of a prairie chicken and never even come close to fulfilling your potential?

Dr. Melvin Lorentzen reminds us that "we must stress excellence over against mediocrity done in the name of Christ. We must determine to put our *best* into the arts, so that when we sing a hymn about Jesus and His love, when we erect a building for the worship of God, when we stage a play about the soul's pilgrimage, we will not repel people but attract them to God."

Perhaps part of our problem is just some defective theology. Many of us have difficulty living with the biblical truth that a sovereign God is doing it all—and the parallel truth that man has not only been given complete responsibility *for* his actions but is commanded to *take action*! This is part of the tension between theology and living, a tension that will never be—nor should it be—resolved. The following story may illustrate what I mean.

A pastor once made an investment in a large piece of ranch real estate which he hoped to enjoy during his years of retirement. While he was still an active pastor, he would take one day off each week to go out to his land and work. But what a job! What he had bought, he soon realized, was several acres of weeds, gopher holes, and run-down buildings. It was anything but attractive, but the pastor knew it had potential and he stuck with it.

Every week he'd go to his ranch, crank up his small tractor, and plow through the weeds with a vengeance. Then he'd spend time doing repairs on the buildings. He'd mix cement, cut lumber, replace broken windows, and work on the plumbing.

It was hard work, but after several months the place began to take shape. And every time the pastor put his hand to some task, he would swell with pride. He knew his labor was finally paying off.

When the project was completed, the pastor received a neighborly visit from a farmer who lived a few miles down the road. Farmer Brown took a long look at the preacher and cast a longer eye over the revitalized property. Then he nodded his approval and said, "Well, preacher, it looks like you and God really did some work here."

The pastor, wiping the sweat from his face, answered, "It's interesting you should say that, Mr. Brown. But I've got to tell you—you should have seen this place when God had it all to Himself!"

It takes action to achieve excellence—deliberate, careful, relentless action. There are no shortcuts to quality.

In his fine book, *Excellence*, John Gardner says, "Some people have greatness thrust upon them. Very few have excellence thrust upon them. . . . They achieve it. They do not achieve it unwittingly by 'doing what comes naturally' and they don't stumble into it in the course of amusing themselves. All excellence involves discipline and tenacity of purpose."

Simple? No. Costly? Yes. Worth it? You bet. But before you take action, and before you move beyond your small ambitions, you need to make some basic decisions. You must know where you are going.

Man, jumping excitedly into taxi: "Quick, do you know how to get to Carnegie Hall?"

Cabbie: "Practice, man, practice."

2

Don't Just Stand There . . . Do Something!

Do what? you ask.

There are so many things to do. How can I possibly decide what is really important for me and my life? How can I be sure that what I *choose* to do is what I really *ought* to do?

Perhaps the simplest advice to you who face this dilemma is *Do something.* Choose a goal and work toward it. Later you may modify it, expand it, or even eventually abandon it for a better one. But first, make a decision. Decide to decide. Or, plan to plan. But don't be like the overenergetic cowboy who raced into the corral, saddled up his bronco, and rode off in all directions.

It may be difficult to choose a specific goal, but

25

unless you do, you may find yourself forever frustrated, nonproductive, and eventually emotionally distraught.

Psychiatrist Ari Kiev of Cornell University, in his fine little book *Strategy for Daily Living,* writes about the importance of *setting a goal* for a person's mental health.

> In my practice as a psychiatrist, I have found that helping people to develop personal goals has proved to be the most effective way to help them to cope with problems. Observing the lives of people who have mastered adversity, I have noted that they have *established goals* and sought with all their effort to achieve them. From the moment they decided to concentrate all their energies on a specific objective, they began to surmount the most difficult odds. . . . The establishment of a goal is the key to successful living.

And we can add that the people who truly excel in their endeavors are invariably the ones who early on (1) determine clear-cut goals and (2) habitually direct all their energies toward fulfilling them. The *decision* to go after a goal is the key to success. The *determination* to stay with it is what brings out the quality of excellence.

Let's take *you* as an example.

Let's say you are a pastor. What are some of your goals?

A Sunday school of five hundred?

A counseling program for all ages in your church?

Your own summer camp?

Two books published in the next three years?

Preparation of four really strong sermons that will stand the test of time?

Obviously you cannot do all these things at once, but what would happen if you took them one at a time? Let's take the goal of writing four truly effective and unforgettable sermons.

Let's say you invested one hour each day, five days a week, toward your goal of producing four great messages. That would be five hours a week, twenty hours a month, two hundred forty hours a year. That's a lot of working hours toward your goal—two hundred forty hours of productive, uninterrupted time. I think you'll agree that with that kind of time spent you could produce some sermons that would become classics.

But what would happen if you were to approach your decision in *this* manner?

> Well, I'd really like to write a few great sermons within the next few years. But I'm still pretty young, and I have lots of time. I think that next summer at the lake would be the perfect time to get moving on the research. Or if that doesn't work out, then maybe I could get started during a couple weekends away next fall.

Good intentions, but will you ever prepare those sermons? Without a conscious decision to start—and finish—will you achieve the quality you want? Will they be truly great? Probably not, because the pursuit of excellence is precisely that—a pursuit! A hot pursuit, if you like, for something you want very much. Dr. Kiev says, "Always have the next goal in the back of your mind, since the most satisfaction comes from *pursuing* a goal, not simply from achieving it."

You may recall the marvelous swimmer, John Naber, who won five gold medals at the Olympic Games in Montreal in 1976. John is a Christian, and it was he who led the victorious American contingent around the Olympic track following the games, triumphantly waving a little American flag.

On his return home to Southern California, he spent an evening in my home church and told of the events of the Montreal Olympics; then he said something that rather startled all of us.

John indicated that following the euphoria of the victories and the adulation he received upon returning home, and after all of the press interviews, he went into deep depression. He knew this wasn't what he ought to feel and sense as a Christian, and he could not figure out what had happened after he had achieved the goals toward which he had worked so hard and so long. He then realized, he reported, that he did not have at that time any other goals beyond winning the Olympic events. As a Christian, he realized that there were better and higher things toward which he needed to strive, and he needed to reset his goals in serving Christ. Recognizing this and facing the situation, he established new goals and testified of the way the Lord met him at this particular point of need.

In contrast, you may recall young speed skater,

Eric Heiden, who, with his sister, was a favorite of the 1980 Olympic Winter Games in Lake Placid, New York. Eric also won his share of gold medals but did not share the problem John Naber faced. Throughout his training and participation, the Olympic wins were simply a step along the way to the achievement of a greater goal—to be a successful surgeon like his father.

Remember, the most satisfaction comes from pursuing the goal, not simply from achieving it!

Remember how Elijah, in the Old Testament, following the stunning victory which God granted to him over the priests of Baal at Mount Carmel, sat under the juniper tree and pouted? He was completely defeated, even though God had given him great victory. Why? At that moment he did not have further direction for his life. But the Lord met him at his point of need, and Elijah went on to further victories in God's name.

As you pursue excellence, you will find that the world around you will have an almost uncanny way of stepping aside when you say, "This is my goal. I am going to reach it." Og Mandino, in his miniature classic *The Greatest Secret in the World*, indicates the importance of sticking with your goal, step by step:

> The prizes of life are at the end of each journey, not near the beginning; and it is not given to me to know how many steps are necessary in order to reach my goal. Failure I may still encounter at the thousandth step, yet success hides behind the next bend in the road. Never will I know how close it lies

unless I turn the corner. . . . I will be likened to the rain drop which washes away the mountain; the ant who devours a tiger; the star which brightens the earth; the slave who builds a pyramid. I will build my castle one brick at a time, for I know that small attempts repeated will complete any undertaking.[1]

Small attempts repeated

One hour a day
Twenty hours a month
Two hundred forty hours a year!

Are you willing to make that kind of commitment toward fulfilling one of your goals? Which of your goals would *not* give up in submission to this kind of relentless discipline?

Many years ago I set a goal, and I set it high. I determined to be the best and most effective manager I could possibly be—not necessarily better than anyone else but better than the Ted Engstrom I saw in the shaving mirror the morning before. What an exciting adventure it has been! I'm sure it is quite obvious to my associates that I haven't always managed well, but I've always *strived* to manage well. My journey is far from over, and I still read everything I can on the subject of management. I read articles, books, specialized magazines, and news clippings. I attend management seminars (and also lecture on the subject several dozen times every year); I spend time with the best management consultants, picking their brains. Every day of my life is another twenty-four hours when I try to manage better than I did the day before. And I'm still learning and seeking to sharpen what I feel is my God-given gift of administration.

An ego trip? I hope not.

A power play to keep others in subjection? Clout? No.

I have simply decided to excel in this one area. And it's a decision for which I thank God daily.

Early in his ministry, the great Bible teacher Martin Lloyd-Jones vowed he would master the Book of Romans. He did. During the years he pastored in the great Westminster Chapel in London he preached through this epistle several times, taking as much as three years at a time to do so, verse by verse, sentence by sentence, word by word, thought by thought. He excelled in his understanding and exposition of this great doctrinal book of the New Testament. Certainly Dr. Jones took to heart Paul's admonition in 1 Corinthians 14:12 (NIV): "Excel in gifts that build up the church"!

History is replete with examples of men and women who changed their world because they dared to accept the challenge of a dream—a goal—of a Mt. Everest . . . a four-minute mile . . . a symphony . . . a *Pilgrim's Progress* . . . a walk on the moon . . . a city reached for God . . . a slum beautified. Augustine, Savonarola, Martin Luther, John Calvin, John Wesley, D. L. Moody, George Washington Carver, Martin Luther King —they all had a dream, a goal. Large ambitions, high goals, great dreams are free to all of us.

And being careful not to exclude the personal, what about goals involving relationships? Your wife, husband, children, employees, co-workers, neighbors?

Dorothy and I have been married for over forty years, and we often remind each other of goal commitments we made even before our marriage, often renewed in the early months, that we would never end a day without the assurance that the lines of communication were open between us and that, as best we knew how, we would "never let the sun go down upon our wrath." Obviously, there have been tensions, healthy arguments, disagreements. I am a scrapper; she's a conciliator. I am feisty, much of the time in a hurry, a perfectionist; she is cool, collected, even-tempered. We're a good match. Our goal has always been to be not only lovers, but best friends, and we have achieved it.

As the children came along and grew into adulthood, we agreed to seek to model this relationship for them. We haven't said, "Here's our goal," but we have been aware of it and trusted osmosis— and the Lord—to reveal it and hopefully transmit it.

What am I saying? A strategy for excellence in our relationships calls for goals which can be measured and accomplished, to which we can refer as benchmarks or guideposts along life's path.

I think we can all take comfort in knowing that

none of us will be judged on the *perfection index.* In the final analysis, the questions to each of us will be: Did you make the most of your talents? Did you work toward developing your potential? Did you choose excellence, or did you coast? Did you rise above the commonplace, or did you survive on mediocrity?

The wisest of all men, Solomon, said: "Whatever your hand finds it to do, do it with all your might." That's ancient wisdom that is desperately needed in today's society, so addicted to the status quo.

Someone has said that the difference between an amateur and professional is about *five minutes more.*

Just five minutes more of reading toward your goal.

Just five minutes more of working out a communication problem with your spouse.

Just five minutes more with a son or daughter who may be having difficulties in school.

Just five minutes more of asking God to give you the special guidance you so desperately need.

Are you an amateur, or are you a professional? Are you willing to give it that extra five minutes? Are you determined to strain your muscles until they cry out for relief, to keep on trying when you want to quit?

Og Mandino writes:

> I will never consider defeat and will remove from my vocabulary such words and phrases as quit, cannot, unable, impossible, out of the question, improbable, failure, unworkable, hopeless and re-

treat: for they are the words of fools. I will avoid despair, but if this disease of the mind should infect me, then I will work on in despair. I will toil and I will endure. I will ignore the obstacles at my feet and keep mine eyes on the goals above my head, for I know that where dry desert ends, green grass grows. . . . I will forget the happenings of the day that is gone, whether they were good or bad, and greet the new sun with confidence that this will be the best day of my life.[2]

If you didn't accomplish all you wanted to today, if you're discouraged and you feel let down by others, just run through the lines of the old song, "Just pick yourself up, dust yourself off, and start all over again."

In the pursuit of excellence, don't just stand there. Do something!

Behold the turtle. He makes progress only when he sticks his neck out.

3

"Mistakes" Are Important

One of the greatest obstacles we face in attempting to reach our potential is the fear of making a mistake, the very human fear of failure. And yet *excellence* is based on failure, usually one failure after another.

The genius inventor Thomas Edison was one day faced by two dejected assistants, who told him, "We've just completed our seven hundredth experiment and we still don't have an answer. We have failed."

"No, my friends," said Edison, "you haven't failed. It's just that we know more about this subject than anyone else alive. And we're closer to finding the answer, because now we know seven hundred things not to do." Edison went on to tell his colleagues, "Don't call it a mistake. Call it an education."

What a marvelous perspective. I don't know how many additional tries it took before Edison achieved success, but we all know that eventually he and his colleagues *did* see the light. Literally.

Whether you are an inventor, a housewife, a student, a pastor, or a business executive, you must adopt the same principle that guided Edison in his laboratory work: Learn from your mistakes and keep going. In fact, don't call them mistakes at all; call them *education*.

I cringe when I recall some of the horrendous mistakes I have made during my lifetime. I have made gross errors in judgment and have been insensitive toward people I really loved. I have unintentionally bruised colleagues and employees. But I've tried to evaluate those mistakes down through the years so that I could learn from them. I hope I have.

I am not alone, however. I am in the company of millions. Because who among us has gone through a single day without committing some error, some mistake?

I'd like you to consider doing this little exercise. Take a few minutes today or tomorrow to carefully observe yourself and people around you. For the sake of this exercise, watch them carefully and see if they make any mistakes. Here's what you may find:

The cashier at the supermarket rings up the

wrong amount for your head of lettuce and has to correct the error on the tape.

The mechanic forgets to tighten that last nut on your car and you leave the repair shop with an annoying rattle in your car.

Your small daughter is learning how to walk and makes mistake after mistake as she forever tumbles to the carpet.

Your spouse is harsh with you over breakfast and in the evening tells you that he/she couldn't wait to put things right.

You inadvertently run a red light and immediately start praying that the police are patrolling in another part of town.

Mistakes. Errors in judgment. Some simple, some critical. As we look around us, we notice that no one is immune. And yet when we look at ourselves, we tend to be mercilessly critical. We speak of ourselves as failures, instead of as having failed in that one task. We're like the proverbial cat who, having sat on one hot stove, swore never to sit on any stove again.

Someone has quipped, "If Thomas Edison had given up that easily, you and I would be watching television in the dark." But he didn't give up, not even after seven hundred "learning experiences." All great discoveries have come about through trial and error. So will yours—whether it's a cure for cancer, a new technique for communicating with teenagers, or a better mousetrap.

I've always been encouraged by the words of Charles Kettering: "You will never stub your toe standing still. The faster you go, the more chance there is of stubbing your toe, but the more chance you have of getting somewhere." And, like the turtle, you really will go nowhere at all unless you stick your neck out. So it's back to our basic decision to *act*. To *do something*. I've heard psychologists say that action—any kind of action—is also a tremendous cure for depression, even if it's no more than a walk around the block.

Today is a good day to start believing that you don't need to live a life of quiet desperation, fearful of any new challenge. Starting today, you can begin to enjoy using and developing your gifts. For a start, you may want to risk something small— like a toe rather than a neck.

For example, if you've always wanted to write, then write something, a short article, a poem, an account of your vacation. Write it as if it were going to be published; then submit it somewhere. If you're a photographer, gather your best pictures together and submit them as entries in a contest. If you think you're a fair tennis player or golfer, enter some tournaments and see how you do. You may not win the top prize, but, think how much you'll learn and experience just by trying.

Or perhaps you've always felt weak in math, or foreign language, or bookkeeping. Enroll today in a basic, nonthreatening course at a local college or a community night school program. The fact that you may have received a poor grade in the subject at 16 has little bearing on how you'll handle the subject matter at age 25, 30, 50, or 65.

Have you wanted to learn to play the piano? You can! Line up an instructor, set up a schedule for lessons, and set aside forty-five minutes a day for practice. In a year you'll be amazed at how well you will do.

Gourmet cooking appeals to you? Get some new recipe books; experiment with one meal each week. So what if the souffle is scorched the first time? The second one will be better. Before you know it, your culinary delights will be lauded and in demand—at least by your family.

Franklin D. Roosevelt once said, "It is common sense to take a method and try it. If it fails, admit it frankly. But above all, *try something*." It's the only way you'll ever begin to realize your God-given potential. And it can be the glorious beginning in your pursuit of a life of excellence.

Don't be afraid of failure. It's by failure that we learn and profit. Ted Williams, one of the greatest baseball batters of all time, failed six times out of ten in his best year when he batted .400! Learn from your failures and mistakes, and move on.

Let me give you two personal examples of how I failed miserably, but how, through sticking with it, made something good of those mistakes.

One Sunday morning, many years ago, I was scheduled to preach in a sizable Indiana church. It was Mother's Day, although I had paid scant attention to that. Upon arriving at the church, the pastor reminded me that it was Mother's Day and said that he hoped I would address the congregation with this particular day in mind. Most unwisely, I agreed that I would. While the congregation sang the hymns, while the choir sang the anthem, and while the ushers received the offering, I prepared a new sermon using the acrostic M-O-T-H-E-R. Rarely has a poorer sermon been preached! I blush to this day as I recall that Sunday morning. But I learned! I learned always to seek the mind of the Lord in preparing a message and, having done this, stick with it. (And never on the spur of the moment.)

On another occasion, I was scheduled to address a large youth rally in Portland, Oregon. I arrived at the meeting utterly fatigued, after traveling and speaking for a number of days and suffering from a severe cold and a splitting headache. Within minutes after beginning to speak, my voice faltered. I began to sound like a croaking frog and finally had no voice at all. I had to sit down in utter defeat, the address barely begun! What did I learn? Get some rest before a message; always have a lozenge available; and make certain that a glass of water is near the pulpit! Thank goodness that experience has not been repeated.

Don't simply commence to get ready to begin to live. Start now. Today. Don't prepare indefinitely to take that course, or teach that Bible class, or ask for that promotion. Do it now. If you're scared to death, admit it. You'll find that the admission alone will quiet your heart and unwrinkle your brow.

Paul Tournier, the well-known Swiss psychiatrist, has said, "God's plan is fulfilled not just through the obedience of inspired men, but also through their errors, yes, their sins."

The Bible is replete with examples of how God turned people's failures—and forgiven sins—into great triumphs. That's His business.

Look, for example, at King David. David failed to discipline his sons, and as a result a whole chain of sorry events occurred. David failed to discipline Amnon after his immoral relationship with his sister, Tamar. This led David's other son, Absalom, to avenge his sister by killing Amnon. Finally, the entire kingdom was totally disrupted when Absalom led a rebellion against his father.

Great warrior that he was, perhaps David lacked what many today are calling "tough love." He had an obvious strong emotional attachment to his children, as when he wept for Absalom after he was killed leading a rebellion, but somehow he could not bring himself to discipline his children as was needed.

We also recognize that David failed to control his physical passions. When David added to his sin with Bathsheba the sin of murder of her husband Uriah, a faithful warrior in his army, he demonstrated a basic character flaw in not being willing to own up to sinful behavior soon enough to avoid adding another sinful act as a coverup.

Yet, despite his great failures, David stands as one of the truly great men of God and of all time. He was a man after God's own heart in his devotion to Him and in his eagerness to honor Him and seek His glory. He did not shake his fist at God after a failure but repented and earnestly prayed that God's spirit would never be taken from him.

Now look at Sarah. In her day, being childless in marriage was often construed as being a failure. A wife's purpose and role were very closely related to rearing children and maintaining the family name and heritage. Sarah had to bear this sense of failure until she was ninety years old. An example of how deeply affected and hurt she was by this sense of failure can be seen in her harsh treatment of Hagar when she was able to bear the child Ishmael. Hagar fled to the wilderness in her despair at Sarah's treatment of her. At the age of ninety, Sarah was undoubtedly a frustrated, disappointed, and bitter woman. It is understandable how she could laugh, though she denied it, when she overheard God telling her husband, Abraham, that she would bear a child. Yet Sarah is listed in the "Hall of Fame of Faith" in Hebrews 11. Her faith grew, and she drew strength from her deep faith in God. The apostle Peter uses her as a key example in his teaching of how wives are to relate to their husbands in honor and obedience (1 Peter 3:6).

Samson is another example: His failures are most evident in his relationship with women. Against the advice of his parents, he chose to marry a woman who evidently did not worship the Lord. This led to much bloodshed between his people and the Philistines and eventually to the death of his wife and her father.

Samson later entered into an immoral relationship with a harlot in the city of Gaza, and the people of that city sought to take his life. And, of course, what follows is the familiar story of the Philistines persuading the beautiful Delilah to entice Samson into telling her where he received his great and unusual strength. He made a game out of the whole situation, leading her along into many false assumptions about the source of his strength. But, finally, persistent Delilah persuaded him to tell her the truth. This led to Samson's capture and imprisonment and eventually to the gouging out of his eyes. Yet, Samson was used greatly by the Lord in helping to rescue Israel from the tyranny of the Philistines. And despite his failures, he was God's man, presiding over and judging the nation of Israel for twenty years.

Turning to the New Testament, we find the apostle Peter, who drew stern rebukes and was told of the shameful denial that he would make of his Lord. At one point, when Jesus was talking about the death that He would die, He perceived that the very thoughts of Satan were coming out of Peter's mouth. And, of course, the three denials of Peter in the course of one evening, disowning any allegiance or association with Jesus, are familiar to all. Though he was irresistibly attracted to being with Jesus, for he knew that He held the very words of life, Peter could not readily accept the ways of Jesus. Even after Jesus had ascended to heaven, Peter had great difficulty in accepting many of the things he had been taught by Jesus. The apostle Paul found it necessary to rebuke Peter and tell him face to face that he was showing prejudice and false standards in dealing with Jews and Gentiles. Yet, who could deny the greatness of Peter, the man who gave pivotal leadership to the early Christian church and was at the forefront of the earliest recorded people movements to Christ. His two New Testament epistles, which relate to bearing up under suffering, have provided great comfort and endurance for Christians throughout the centuries. His loyalty and devotion to Jesus Christ in his latter years have been an inspiration to all believers for two millenia.

And finally, there is Jonah. The reluctance of Jonah to do what God had asked him to do stands out as a glaring example of great stubbornness and rebellion, and perhaps fear. His was no passive resistance, but rather an active effort to get as far away from the place and purpose of God as possible. He was told to go to the great city of Nineveh and proclaim God's great displeasure with the wicked and godless ways of the people there. When Jonah finally got turned around, in a most unusual manner, and did what he was told to do, he displayed a selfish anger with God and the people of Nineveh. Rather than rejoicing that they had repented and were responding favorably to God, he displayed a great deal of contempt and selfish anger toward both God and the Ninevites. Then Jonah went outside the city gates, and in his despair—and perhaps exhaustion—asked that his life might be taken.

Still, Jonah remains one of the great examples of

a man delivered and used by God, almost in spite of himself. It is recorded that a whole city of people, favorably affected by Jonah's preaching, turned away from their sins. And Jonah's prayer for deliverance, one of the great prayers of the Bible, was even quoted by the Lord Jesus Christ in His earthly ministry.

God does not expect perfection; He expects obedience. And through obedience He can turn failures into triumphs.

Each of these Bible characters was unique. So are you. Develop your own style. No one has had the life experiences you have had; no one has the contributions to make that *you* can make. So it's not a question of being better than someone else. Excellence demands that you be better than yourself.

Some people are outgoing, while others are introspective. Some are thinkers rather than doers. Some are leaders; some are followers. Some are ahead of their times; many are behind. Some are musical geniuses; most are not. Some are great preachers; many are not. But whatever category you are in, right now you can make that single, deliberate move toward a life of excellence.

We are all aware of true and challenging illustrations of hosts of people who have triumphantly overcome seemingly impossible handicaps and disabilities. Let me illustrate with just two familiar and moving examples. The first is my friend Joni Eareckson.

At the age of eighteen, Joni became paralyzed

from the neck down after a diving accident in shallow water at Chesapeake Bay. She had total quadriplegia, the result of a diagonal fracture between the fourth and fifth cervical levels.

Joni survived the critical first few weeks but soon came to the point of total despair and frequently wanted to commit suicide. Her reasons were understandable. Her appearance was grotesque—at least to her. Her weight had dropped from 125 to 80 pounds, her skin was jaundiced, her head had to be shaved to help hold her in a brace, and her teeth had become black from medication. Added to that was her sense of extreme limitations and her fear of the future. However, she let Christ turn that tragedy into triumph, those limitations into unlimited opportunities, and her fear into fortitude.

She has since done some utterly remarkable things. For example, she learned to draw and paint by holding a pen or brush in her teeth, and her work is truly remarkable. She refused to remain cloistered, and began accepting numerous speaking engagements, including appearances on television programs such as the "Today" show. As a result she has spoken to tens of thousands of people, telling her story and encouraging them to find the hope and purpose which a life in Jesus Christ makes possible. And she has developed a ministry called Joni and Friends, which seeks to encourage others who are handicapped and to increase the understanding of those not handicapped.

The second person I want to remind you of is Helen Keller. At the age of nineteen months, because of illness, Helen became totally blind and deaf and speechless. Needless to say, it would have seemed that she had no future.

But Helen was a highly spirited girl and was tremendously encouraged by the loving care of her mother. When Helen was seven, the "beloved teacher," as Helen called her, came into her life. Anne Mansfield Sullivan was greatly responsible for unleashing in Helen Keller the great desire to express herself.

Through Anne's help, Helen went on to graduate cum laude from Radcliffe College. Helen had been determined to attend college years earlier, and it was due to her own insistence that she was finally enrolled. Devoting her life to helping others deprived of sight and sound, she traveled all over the world on their behalf, giving lectures. She wrote several articles and books, including an autobiography. Her contribution was such that Mark Twain said that the two most interesting characters of the nineteenth century were Napoleon and Helen Keller.

What about you? Whether *your* handicap is physical or emotional, today can be the day you begin to chip away at that granite mountain of self-defeat. You can read books about how to do it. You can attend seminars on assertiveness training. You can discuss your plans for change with your friends and pray about it until the cows come home. But ultimately it's up to you to take action.

And to take action that is productive you must know who you are . . . and what you are. It is my hope that today you will recognize that God made you in a special way for His special purpose. He wants you to be all He meant you to be. And He wants you to perform with class.

It was said of Jesus, "Behold, He does all things well." A Jesus of mediocrity, a Jesus of the average, is not the Jesus of the Bible. And if we want a model of one who took risks and lived a life of excellence, we can find none better than the life of our Lord.

He confronted the religious leaders of His day, mincing no words. (Very risky).

He claimed to be the Son of God. (This ultimately cost Him His life.)

He took a whole series of shopworn religious legal statements and suggested that they could best be summed up as: Love your God, and love your neighbor as yourself. (Tampering with sacred tradition.)

He spent huge amounts of time with so-called second-class citizens: tax collectors, prostitutes, lepers, disabled, Samaritans. (Misguided indeed.)

He was furious when His Father's house was turned into a noisy marketplace. (Tampering with temple economics.)

He had the audacity to reach out and heal the sick on the Sabbath. (Couldn't He lay off for just one day?)

He encouraged the little children to come to His side so He could tell them He loved them, too.

(Judea was hardly a child-centered society.)

And during His last days on earth, He chose to love those who persecuted Him, mocked Him, and exposed Him to every human indignity imaginable.

During the later part of His earthly ministry Jesus also said that His followers—you and I—would do greater things than He had done. Have you ever wondered if He really meant that? If He did, then we need His discipline and His courage. We need His anger at injustice and His untiring concern for those who suffer. We need His capacity for taking risks. And we need to know more of His great love.

I hold a doctrine to which I owe
much, indeed, but all the little I
ever had, namely, that with ordi-
nary talent and extraordinary
perserverance, all things are at-
tainable.

T.F. Buxton

4

How High Is Your AQ—
Your Attitude Quotient?

One day a man who took great pride in his lawn
found himself with a large healthy crop of dande-
lions. He tried every conceivable method he knew
to get rid of them, but they still plagued him and
his lawn. Finally, he wrote to the Department of
Agriculture, enumerating all the things he had
tried, and closed his letter with the question,
"What shall I do now?" In due course came the
reply, "We suggest you learn to love them."[1]

Each of us faces people and situations every day
that exasperate us. And often, despite our hercu-
lean efforts, the exasperation simply won't go
away. It's then we realize that perhaps the biggest
risk of all is *changing our attitude*.

In a recent lecture, Jim Rohn of Adventure in Achievement shared these observations on what he called the "diseases of attitude":

Indifference: The mild approach to life. Don't let this rob you of the good life.

Indecision: The greatest thief of opportunity. A life of adventure is a life filled with many decisions— good ones and bad ones.

Doubt: One of the worst is self-doubt. Turn the coin over. *Belief* is a better gamble than doubt.

Worry: The real killer. Worry in its final stages can reduce you to begging. It causes health problems and financial problems.

Overcaution: Some people will never have much. They're just too cautious. Let the record book show you won, or let it show you lost, but don't let it show you failed to play the game.

A recurrent theme in Rohn's lecture was this: *The major key to your better future is you*. Not your boss, not your salary, not your "situation," but *you*.

I guess at times we all wish things were easier. We wish interest rates would come down so we could buy our dream home. We wish our children would start to appreciate all we've done for them. We wish we could just coast once in a while on our way to a life of excellence. And sometimes we just have a large umbrella wish that life would be a bit fairer to us.

Well, we can wish all we want. We can dream pipe dreams of a utopia where the other guy does all the work and where we get all the money and all the credit. But that's all it will ever be—a dream, because there's an ancient law that is still powerfully in effect. It's as old as the farmer who put that first seed into the earth thousands of years ago. *You reap what you sow.*

If you don't like the crops that are coming up all around your feet, you may want to check and see what you're planting these days: Cabbage still gives cabbage, and apples still produce apples. A smile breeds a smile. Negative thoughts stimulate the growth of more negative thoughts.

This law is as old as the hills, and as far as I know, the cleverest attorney has yet to find a loophole. So it's probably best not to try to beat the system. Instead, if you don't like what you see, check your bag of seeds—the seeds of attitudes— and determine what you've been growing in your emotional garden.

Let me illustrate this "sowing and reaping" law from the Scriptures:

Haman was a high official of the court of King Ahasuerus (Xerxes of Persia) who became furious when a Jew named Mordecai refused to bow down to him, as the king had commanded. Thus, Haman set out to destroy Mordecai and all the other Jews in Persia. He even prepared an unusually tall (seventy-five feet) gallows for Mordecai.

As it turned out, the queen, Esther, was also a Jew and was the cousin of Mordecai. At a special dinner which she prepared for the king and Haman, she revealed Haman's evil plot to the king. The king became furious and ordered that Haman and his sons be hanged on the very same gallows which Haman had prepared for Mordecai and that the Jews would take up arms to defend themselves against any who were seeking to harm them under Haman's previous plans. Here we see one of the most ironic biblical examples of the principle of sowing and reaping.

We can also see in the life and reign of King Solomon the results and rewards of a kingdom founded on the righteous reign of his father, King David. In David's forty years as ruler of Israel, he sought to build his kingdom on the foundation of God's statutes, commandments, and ordinances.

Solomon, gifted by God as the wisest man ever to live, ruled over all the kingdoms from the Euphrates to the land of the Philistines and to the border of Egypt. To Solomon was given the great privilege of building the house and temple of the Lord in all its magnificence. Solomon sought to be diligent in following the Lord, as did his father David. We see this in his benediction prayer for the newly completed temple, in which he says: "May the Lord maintain the cause of his servant, and the cause of his people Israel . . . that all the peoples of the earth may know that the Lord is God; there is no other."

The life of Solomon is an example of reaping positive results from the very positive sowing done earlier by his father David and by himself.

Joseph is another positive example of the sowing and reaping principle. Abandoned to a desert well to die, sold into slavery by his brothers, falsely accused of adultery by his master's wife, and finally cast into prison, Joseph remained faithful to God. He continued to give God credit for his abilities and special insight. God rewarded Joseph's faithfulness, and Joseph became a ruler under Pharaoh and was instrumental in helping the entire nation of Egypt to survive a famine of seven years, as well as in assisting his family through those famine years.

Finally, think of the story of Ananias and Sapphira in the Book of Acts. To lie to another human being is a sinful deed, but to lie to God Himself has awesome consequences; and it cost this couple their very lives.

They said that all the proceeds from the piece of property which they had sold were going into the Lord's work among the early apostles, when in fact they were keeping some of the money for their own use. Each was questioned separately about the land sale and whether or not their claim about giving all of it was true. They each chose to lie about money which they were withholding for themselves, and both, as they finished their statement of falsehood, were immediately struck dead. This is one of the most dramatic examples in the Scriptures of instant consequences resulting from a sin. They immediately reaped the results of the lie they had sown. While we do not often see this sowing and reaping principle so readily apparent, it continues to operate!

Let me ask you a question. Do you know any grumps? I mean real bona-fide grumps—the kind who frown, mumble incessantly, belittle others, and walk about with a little gray cloud forever hanging over their drooping heads? Not much fun to be with, are they? They are afflicted with a disease of attitude. By six o'clock each morning they already *know* it's going to be a lousy day!

And then there are our friends who always seem to be "up," pleasant, interesting, and interested. They are, in contrast, a joy to be around. Their warmth and good humor are contagious. They have the capacity to share their gift of encouragement with everyone they meet. Their attitudes are healthy.

One of the ingredients for a life of excellence is just that—healthy attitudes. One smile is still worth a hundred frowns in any market.

A smile
- costs nothing but creates much.
- enriches those who receive without diminishing the wealth of those who give.
- happens in a flash, but the memory of it can last a lifetime. None are so rich that they can get along without it and none so poor but are richer for it.
- creates happiness in the home, fosters good will in a business, and is the countersign of friends.
- is rest to the weary, daylight to the discouraged, and nature's best antidote for trouble.
- cannot be bought, begged, or stolen, for it is of no earthly good to anybody until it is given away.

- And if any person should be too tired to give you a smile, why not give one of your own?
- For nobody needs a smile so much as one who has none to give.[2]

Charles Schwab, the man to whom Andrew Carnegie paid a million dollars a year because of his ability to motivate people, once said, "A man can succeed at almost anything for which he has unlimited enthusiasm." Show me a person who has that approach to life, and I'll show you a man or woman who has attitudes that are positive and constructive.

One of my heroes, Theodore Roosevelt, said this about attitudes:

> It is not the critic who counts: not the man who points out how the strong man stumbled or where the doer of deeds could have done them better. The credit belongs to the man who is actually in the arena; whose face is marred by dust and sweat and blood; who strives valiantly; who errs, and comes short again and again, because there is no effort without error and shortcomming; who does actually try to do the deed; who knows the great enthusiasm, the great devotion, and spends himself in a worthy cause; who, at the worst, if he fails, at least fails while daring greatly.
>
> Far better it is to dare mighty things, to win glorious triumphs even though checkered by failure, than to rank with those poor spirits who neither enjoy nor suffer much because they live in the gray twilight that knows neither victory nor defeat.

That "gray twilight" zone of mediocrity is no place for a person committed to a life of excellence—and certainly no place for a child of God.

Following a serious World War II accident which involved a shattered hip, I was told I would have limited leg mobility and a noticeable limp and undoubtedly would have played my last game of golf, which was my favorite recreation and sport. It was a devastating announcement. But I determined that bad hip or no, I was once again going to enjoy golf.

Three surgeries later, with a rehabilitated and rebuilt hip and a lift on my right spiked golf shoe, I play eighteen holes with regularity (almost as often as I wish I could!).

It's the "attitude quotient" that counts!

We began this chapter by talking about what Rohn called "diseases of attitude." But what are the cures for those ailments of the spirit? How can we bring our attitudes back to a state of healthy well-being? Let's take them one at a time.

Indifference: The most effective cure for this "mild approach to life" is to get excited about something. Point yourself in one direction and move toward it. It could be anything from being the best gardener on the block to running an effective organization. But you will *never* know the thrill of the hunt until you get yourself worked up about something. Today, start putting everything you've got into everything you do. It's the perfect cure for this killer disease.

Indecision: The antidote for indecision is simple. In fact, we've already talked about it in chapter two: *Don't just stand there . . . do something!* Get off the dime and get a move on. You don't have to discover the cure for some rare disease. Your decision may simply be to read a book on how to further your career, or it may be patching up a relationship that is significant to you.

Doubt: This is the greatest killer of all. Especially self-doubt. The Scriptures tell us not to think overly impressive thoughts of ourselves. But they also encourage us to think realistically about our strengths, abilities, gifts, and talents. The cure for self-doubt is belief—not a blind allegiance toward doing the improbable, but a healthy belief in ourselves and in the gifts God has so generously given to each of us. That includes *you*. Everyone has God-given gifts. What are yours?

Worry: The Word of God is such a comfort if we will but choose to believe what it tells us. First Peter 5:7 reads, "Casting all your care on him, for he cares for you." I can think of no greater assault on the problem of worry than to quietly take our pain and frustration and place them at the feet of the Savior. Among the most visible benefits may even be a reduction in your lower back pain or fewer attacks of peptic ulcers.

Overcaution: This is the "what if" syndrome. You've been there. *What if* I speak up and declare my own point of view on this issue? I might lose some friends in the process. *What if* I decide to do something nice for myself, like buy a car or take a long trip? "They" might think I'm selfish. *What if* I buy a new home, get saddled with high payments, and then lose my job? I can't prove it statistically, but I would be willing to wager that 95 percent of our worries *never ever* come to pass.

The opposite side of timidity and overcaution is adventure—taking risks and accepting challenges that are beyond your immediate ability to deliver. This is what a life of excellence is all about.

But these diseases of attitude are always lurking, always ready to infest and infect the garden of your mind. So be on guard. Keep sowing attitudes that are constructive, that will bring you a step closer each day to the goals you have set for yourself. It's part of the pursuit of excellence. And it will help keep you from being afflicted with that most dread of all diseases—the status quo (which someone has said is Latin for "the mess we're in"!).

Mediocrity is excellent to the eye
of the mediocre.
                    Joubert

5

You Don't Have
to Be Average

I wonder how many of you would have bought this book if the title had been *HOW TO BE BELOW AVERAGE*, or *HOW I ACHIEVED MEDIOCRITY*, or *HOW I GOT TO BE LESS THAN THE BEST*! Oh, you may have leafed through a few pages just to see what kind of a crackpot had put the volume together, but I seriously doubt if many would have chosen to make the investment. After all, who among us needs any encouragement to be average? For millions that's already the problem. The majority of people in our country live every day beneath their God-given potential. Instead of responding to life's challenges with personal growth and a commitment to specific goals, they are addicted to a dead-end status quo.

Beginning today, you can move beyond that dismal gray existence of mediocrity and start exploring new heights. But this new adventure will begin only with your personal commitment to becoming better than you have known or seen yourself to be.

When Britain's late, great prime minister, Sir Winston Churchill, was a young teenager, he attended a public school called Harrow. Young Winston was not a good student; as a matter of fact, he was quite a rascal. Had he not been the son of the famed Lord Randolph Churchill, he probably would have been expelled from the school. However, he completed his work at Harrow, went on to the university, and then embarked on a brilliant and illustrious career in the British military, serving in both Africa and India.

At age sixty-seven, he was elected prime minister of the British Empire. It was he who brought great courage to the nation through his speeches and leadership during the dark days Britain faced in World War II.

Toward the very end of his leadership as prime minister, the old statesman was invited to address the young boys at his alma mater, Harrow. In announcing the coming of their great leader, the headmaster said, "Young gentlemen, the greatest orator of our time—perhaps of all time—our prime minister, will be here in a few days to address you; and it will behoove you to listen carefully to whatever sound advice he may bring to you at that time."

The great day arrived, and the prime minister appeared at Harrow. Following a glowing and lengthy introduction by the headmaster, Sir Winston stood up—all five feet, five inches and 235 pounds of him! After he had acknowledged the effusive introduction, he gave this brief but moving speech: "Young men, never give up. Never give up! Never give up!! Never, never, never, never!"

Start "not giving up" right now. Today. And one of the best ways to get started is to begin observing those who seem to be better than average.

When Dr. Elton Trueblood was a student at Harvard, his mentor, Dean Sperry, said to him, "You must have some great models." That's when Trueblood realized that the real enemy is mediocrity and that he should seek excellence. And he realized that the way to seek excellence was to soak his life with characters who had achieved excellence.

These may be community leaders, pastors, housewives, teachers, parents, or co-workers. Watch them carefully. Talk with them. Find out what they read. Explore their interests. Talk to people who work with those who are excelling in their occupations and in their personal lives. Give careful attention to their style. If a person is making $80,000 a year, perhaps he or she has an $80,000 smile. Perhaps that person has learned how to listen better than anyone else around.

Success leaves clues. And as you carry out this private research, I think you'll also discover that achievers are not born. They are made. The same can be said for underachievers—for the average man or woman.

As you observe those who excel, be on the lookout for specific qualities that set them apart, qualities you would like to implement in your own life. Qualities such as the following:

Personal discipline: Those who excel are people who, first of all, take charge of themselves. They plan their work and then they work their plan. They are neither burning out nor coasting along; they have achieved a balance in their lives. They know they have physical, emotional, intellectual, and spiritual needs; and they see to it that those needs are met.

Vision: Above-average people have developed the foresight to see how things will work out as a result of their policies and methods. They are always looking ahead, so they also have the insight to make good decisions.

Optimism: People who excel are not "downers." Of course they have their moments of discouragement, but for the most part they respond to life with a cheerful spirit and an attitude that "this problem can be solved." An optimist laughs to forget; a pessimist forgets to laugh! The pessimist sees a difficulty in every opportunity and the optimist sees an opportunity in every difficulty.

A sense of adventure: Above-average people create their own adventures and engineer a large measure of their own happiness. These people take risks, push themselves to the limit, and stretch their minds and bodies in pursuit of their goals.

Courage: Above-average people know that it is always too soon to quit. That excellence demands courage in the face of defeat. Many games have been won in the bottom of the ninth because of *one* pitch-hit single. The highest degree of courage is seen in the people who are most fearful but refuse to let fear defeat them. However fearful they may have been, God's leaders in every generation have been commanded to be of good courage. Remember God's word to Joshua, "Be strong and of good courage. . . . I will not fail you nor forsake you."

Humility: People of excellence do not talk excessively about themselves or their many accomplishments. They are content to let their track records do the talking. More than likely, you will have to pry stories of great achievements out of them. The apostle Paul said in 1 Corinthians 15, "I am the least of the apostles, and do not even deserve to be called an apostle."

Humor: Above-average people know that "a merry heart does good like a medicine." Humor can relax the most difficult of situations and create an atmosphere of good-will. Perhaps one of the most outstanding qualities of above-average people is their ability to laugh at themselves. A good laugh at oneself is better than a tonic. It saves many difficult situations.

Confidence: People of excellence know that if they don't believe in themselves, no one else will believe in them either. Self-confidence is not unspiritual. Quite the contrary, it is an honest belief in the gifts and talents given to you by God.

Anger: Above-average people are healthy enough to get angry, but angry at the right things—like injustice, incompetence (especially in themselves), and poor use of time and money. This quality of anger was present in our Lord when He swept the moneychangers from the temple and when He spoke so harshly of the ancient laws that had such little regard for people. The apostle Paul said, "Be angry, but sin not."

Patience: Above-average people are patient. They are careful listeners. Only after all the facts are in do they make a decision.

Integrity: A life of excellence is one which has trustworthiness as its base. Above-average people can be trusted. Their word means something. They can be counted on to deliver. They have a deep sense of personal responsibility. They will not cheat on themselves, their family, or their work.

Finally, being above average is not dependent upon race, age, or sex.

Babe Ruth had hit 714 home runs during his baseball career and was playing one of his last full major league games. It was the Braves versus the Reds in Cincinnati. But the great Ruth was no longer as agile as he had once been. He fumbled the ball and threw badly, and in one inning alone his errors were responsible for most of the five runs scored by Cincinnati.

As the Babe walked off the field after the third out and headed toward the dugout, a crescendo of yelling and booing reached his ears. Just then a boy jumped over the railing onto the playing field.

With tears streaming down his face, he threw his arms around the legs of his hero.

Ruth didn't hesitate for one second. He picked up the boy, hugged him, and set him down on his feet, patting his head gently. The noise from the stands came to an abrupt halt. Suddenly there was no more booing. In fact, hush fell over the entire park. In those brief moments, the fans saw two heroes: Ruth, who in spite of his dismal day on the field could still care about a little boy; and the small lad, who cared about the feelings of another human being. Both had melted the hearts of the crowd.[1]

That's being above average!

> Most people die before they are
> fully born. Creativeness means to
> be born before one dies.
>
> Eric Fromm

6

A Creative Attitude

You and I walk the halls of the great Smithsonian Institution in Washington, D.C., and we overhear ourselves say, "My, we are obviously seeing the handiwork of some of the inventive geniuses of our age."

We travel to Europe and move past row upon row of paintings and sculptures in the Louvre in Paris, and we know we are viewing the work of the world's true creative giants—Rembrandt, Van Gogh, Michelangelo, Rodin and many others.

But whether it's a time-honored museum that houses the world's great art treasures or an afternoon of sidewalk art in Santa Monica, Phoenix, or Chicago, we are never far from the artistic talent of men and women we have labeled "creative." On canvas, on the printed page, in the concert hall, on the movie screen, their work is everywhere.

But I would like to suggest that we give the word *creative* a somewhat wider berth, one that will include not only the renowned artistic geniuses of our time, but also you and me. I'm referring to expanding the idea of *creative* into the larger concept of a *creative attitude*, an attitude that says, "I am willing to be 'fully born,' to abandon the secure certainties of life, and to part company with my many illusions. I will live a life of faith and courage, even if it means aloneness and 'being different.' "

The Bible is full of examples of courage to challenge us. Think, for example, of Abraham. Abraham displayed courage by doing what God had told him to do, even though the outcome was unclear and uncertain. Abraham was told to leave his home in Haran and go in the general direction of Canaan, not certain exactly of where he was going. And this at the age of 75! All that he had was the promise from God that He would lead him and that He would make of him a great nation. Not only was Abraham at an age when tearing up familiar roots of family and friends would be particularly difficult, but also he did not yet have any children of his own from which a nation could emerge. It should be noted also that Abraham was a very rich man, and so he was not motivated by economic necessity to move on to "greener pastures" in order to survive and make a better living. It was simply a matter of believing God and having the courage to translate that belief into the action necessary to see a promise of God fulfilled.

Young Daniel's courage had to do with the very essence of what it means to worship the Lord God and none other. He had the courage of his convictions, choosing to stay true to his devotion to the Lord rather than to continue living and compromise his commitment to almighty God. The issue was whether or not Daniel would take thirty days off from any outward display of prayer to God, so that the only prayers offered would be to King Darius. After all, some would say, he could still pray secretly in his heart and not show any physical sign of praying to God and thereby feign obedience to the edict from the king. But this was not for Daniel. He knew the intention of the edict, and he would have nothing to do with it. Though it could cost him his life, he would not give dual devotion and worship to God and the king. His courage was rewarded with deliverance from a den of lions, but he was well-prepared to pay with his life for his convictions.

Or think of Moses. There is a brief account in the Book of Exodus which displays the physical courage of Moses. (Of the two, physical and moral courage, most say that moral courage is the most difficult; but examples of physical courage are much-needed in our day when soft and comfortable living may ill prepare us for displaying it.)

One day Moses was sitting by a well where seven daughters were attempting to water their father's sheep. Some shepherds came and drove them away, evidently not willing to wait their turn and knowing that the women were not capable of opposing them. "Moses got up and came to their rescue (the women) and watered their flock" (Exod. 2:17). Though outnumbered, Moses opposed those men, standing up for the oppressed women.

The man named Saul had been breathing threats and murder against the early disciples of Jesus Christ. He would literally drag men and women from their houses and commit them to prison because of their Christian faith.

This same Saul had a dramatic conversion to Christianity, became Paul, and began to proclaim to others this new life in Christ. He wanted to fellowship with the Christians in Jerusalem, but the Christians there were afraid and distrustful of him. They just could not believe that their enemy was really a Christian now. However, there was one man who was willing to stick his neck out and proclaim that Paul's conversion was genuine. This man was Barnabas. "Barnabas took him (Paul) and brought him to the apostles" (Acts 9:27). It takes courage to get involved in a controversial issue and take up the defense of someone whom most or all of your friends and close associates oppose. Barnabas did and was instrumental in helping to launch Paul's career as a missionary-statesman throughout Europe and Asia Minor. This one act of courage was important in gaining the support of the Jerusalem believers, which Paul needed as he began his new role as an apostle of Jesus Christ.

These obviously were creatively courageous people. To be truly creative means much more than painting a picture, or writing a play, or inventing a machine. Creativity has been built into every one of us; it's part of our design. Each of us lives less of the life God intended for us when we choose not to live out the creative powers we possess.

John Gardner, in his modern classic *Self Renewal*, says:

> Exploration of the full range of his own potentialities is not something that the self-renewing man leaves to the chances of life. It is something he pursues systematically, or at least avidly, to the end of his days. He looks forward to an endless and unpredictable dialog between his potentialities and claims of life—not only the claims he encounters but the claims he invents. And by potentialities I mean not just the skills but the full range of his capacities for sensing, wondering, learning, understanding, loving and aspiring.[1]

Gardner is right. But you may have fallen into the trap of believing that creativity is only for the other person. Not so. A life of richness awaits you, whether you ultimately hang a painting in the Smithsonian, or whether you become the best mother or father it's possible for you to become.

In *The Self in Pilgrimage*, Earl A. Loomis, Jr. asks an important question: "Why are we afraid to embrace our virtues? Why do we mask them behind inaccurate estimates and unreasonable fears?" He then suggests this answer: "Basically we resist recognition of our assets because once recognized they must be *used*."

What is more tormenting than recognizing a potential and then refusing to put it to work? It's like possessing a miracle drug capable of saving the lives of thousands but keeping it in a locked vault.

What is more personally tragic than love unused? Generosity kept to oneself? Friendship unshared? The world's literature is filled with tales of men and women who knew their own potential, recognized their own talents but refused to use those gifts. Consequently, they are the truly tragic figures of history. It would be far better not to know of a gift than to be aware of it and refuse to use it.

I was cleaning out a little desk drawer the other day when I found a flashlight I'd not used for over a year. I turned it on but was not surprised when it gave no light. I unscrewed it and shook it to get the batteries out, but they wouldn't budge. Finally, after some effort, they came loose. What a mess! Battery acid had corroded the entire inside of the flashlight. The batteries were new when I put them in a year before, and I certainly had stored the flashlight in a safe, warm, comfortable place. But there was one problem. Those batteries were not built to be warm and comfortable. They were designed to be turned on—to be used. That was their only reason for existing.

It's the same with us. You and I were made to be "turned on"—to put our love to work, to apply our patience in difficult, trying situations. We are called upon to take the energies God has given us and compel them to do productive labor for ourselves and others. *This* is what it means to be creative. This is what is means to be *fully born*.

Right now, is there an attitude, a skill, or a talent in your life that is wasting away? Are you letting it disintegrate, atrophy?

It's easy to coast. But except for cream, I know nothing else of quality that floats to the top. A life of excellence takes work, perseverence, and discipline; but it's worth every ounce of sweat and determination. If you choose to let your talents slide, be ready to accept the harsh verdict of that ancient law: What you refuse to use, you will surely lose.

And if you fail at one pursuit, don't become a recluse. Life has not come to an end. It's not what happens that's critical. *It's what you do about what happens* that's important.

The apostle Paul spent months in prison, in Philippi, Rome, and elsewhere. His prison epistles have inspired millions for over two millennia. In the darkest night, in the most desperate of circumstances, his bright, cheerful outlook encouraged the early church, and these letters continue to encourage the church today.

Mother Teresa, who has become a legendary humanitarian figure in our time, was born of impoverished Albanian parents in Yugoslavia. Albania, where there has been no public worship of any kind for decades, is the most hard-core Communist nation in Eastern Europe. Yugoslavia is likewise a part of the atheistic Communistic society. From such an unlikely background came this beautiful person who ministers grace, lovingkindness, and mercy to the destitute and dying in Calcutta, the dirtiest, filthiest city in Asia. She is loved by the mighty and the lowly alike. Visit her Home of Mercy next to the wretched Kali Temple in the heart of the slums of this slum city, as I have, and you will encounter a slice of heaven on earth. Here, because of Mother Teresa's concern and care, the beggars, the indigent, and the homeless die with dignity—and the word whispered in their ears is that God loves them!

My friend, Tom Skinner, black Harlem gang leader, tough and ready to battle with the lifting of a knife, met the Savior through the loving witness of a friend and today ministers the gospel to thousands of university students, conducts large and effective community-wide crusades, and heads up one of the most effective evangelism efforts in our nation today.

The apostle Paul, Mother Teresa, Tom Skinner —and thousands of others with the most unpretentious of backgrounds or unlikely circumstances have made a difference in their world. They pursue excellence, for Christ's sake. So can you and I.

Background, education, circumstances . . . none of these can hold back a creative spirit.

Think, for example, of Abraham Lincoln, who was elected president of the United States in 1860. He grew up on an isolated farm and had only one year of formal education. In those early years, he was exposed to barely half a dozen books. In 1832 he lost his job and was defeated in the race for the Illinois legislature. In 1833 he failed in business. In 1834 he was elected to the state legislature, but in 1835 his sweetheart died, and in 1836 he had a nervous breakdown. In 1838 he was defeated for Speaker of the House, and in 1843 he was defeated for nomination for Congress. In 1846 he was elected to Congress but in 1848 lost the renomination. In 1849 he was rejected for a federal land officer appointment, and in 1854 he was defeated for the Senate. In 1856 he was defeated for the nomination of vice president, and in 1858 he was again defeated for the Senate.

Many people, both at home and abroad, consider Lincoln to be the greatest president of all time. Yet it should be remembered how many failures and defeats marked his life and how humble and unpromising his early beginnings were.

Martin Luther was born into the peasant class, his father a poor mine worker. The peasants were considered to be the most religiously conservative element of the general population. Roland Bainton said that there was "nothing whatever to set Luther off from his contemporaries, let alone to explain why later on he should have revolted against so much of medieval religion." Luther was a common man, and he entered the monastic life in order to make his peace with God and with a more than ordinary devotion to follow the way prescribed by the church. Yet Luther began a protest for reform which shook the very foundations of

Western civilization, and some point to the days of Luther as the beginning of modern times. Even within the Catholic church today, there are leaders who are grateful to Luther for the reforms which he helped stir within the church itself.

Shirley Chisholm, the strong, black congresswoman from the Bedford-Stuyvesant section of Brooklyn, came from a family that was very poor. Both of her parents worked when they could, her mother as a seamstress and her father as an unskilled laborer in a burlap bag factory.

Shirley was a bright child and did well in school. She graduated from Brooklyn College and intended to be a teacher, but she became increasingly angry at the injustices she saw around her and decided she would have to fight the system, "even if I had to stand alone." She eventually entered politics as a congresswoman, thereby becoming the first black woman to serve in Congress.

Shirley knew that Congress was badly in need of reform and that their priorities must be changed. She was convinced that a great number of the leaders in Congress were out of touch, out of tune, with the country. Her first assignment as a congresswoman from an urban constituency was a seat on the Agricultural Committee! She challenged the House leadership before the Democratic caucus and won. They changed their minds and asked her to serve on the Veterans Committee, which was at least relevant to many of her districts.

Shirley Chisholm credits her grandmother for much of her philosophy today:

> She always used to say "You must have courage and conviction, and remember that when you take a stand on things in this world, quite often you are going to find yourself alone. . ." She imprinted on my mind the necessity to fight for that in which you believe, even though you may not always have supporters.

Shirley Chisholm credits the church with having a terrific influence in giving her stamina and strength.

> When I am disillusioned, all I have to do is get on my knees and pray, and in ten minutes I seem to have gotten a new lease of life. I get a kind of inner strength from God. I don't seem to need anybody to stand with me in what I do. The only thing I want and need is to look to my conscience—and God.

Much of her standing alone has been in her fight against injustice toward black people in her district. And her word to those who are black and poor in her district is to make education the number one priority and to "realize that the world has no room for weaklings, and that it is only weaklings who give up in the face of obstacles."

Do you feel that if only your circumstances would change, then you could work on your creativity? Nonsense. The "perfect" environment hasn't been invented yet—and probably never will be.

Once again, look around you at the people whom

you admire for their lives of excellence. What do you see? More than likely, you will see many of the following traits.

1. Drive—a high degree of motivation
2. Courage—tenacity and persistence
3. Goals—a sense of direction
4. Knowledge—and a thirst for it
5. Good health
6. Honesty—especially intellectual
7. Optimism
8. Judgment
9. Enthusiasm
10. Chance-taking—the willingness to risk failure
11. Dynamism—health and energy
12. Enterprise—willing to tackle tough jobs
13. Persuasion—ability to sell
14. Outgoingness—friendly
15. Communication—articulate
16. Receptive—alert
17. Patient yet impatient—patient with others yet impatient with the status quo
18. Adaptability—capable of change
19. Perfectionism—seeking to achieve excellence
20. Humor—ability to laugh at self and others
21. Versatility—broad interests and skills
22. Curiosity—interested in people and things
23. Individualism—self-esteem and self-sufficiency
24. Realism-idealism—occupied by reality but guided by ideals.
25. Imagination—seeking new ideas, combinations, and relationships.[2]

None of the above comes easy, not even for the geniuses of our world.

J.C. Penney once observed, "Geniuses themselves don't talk about the gift of genius. They just talk about hard work and long hours."

Edison believed that genius was 1 percent inspiration and 99 percent perspiration.

Paderewski, when called a genius, said, "Perhaps, but before I was a genius I was a drudge."

So if at first you don't succeed, try and try again. Remember, it took Thomas Edison over seven hundred attempts before he saw the light.

Start today! Develop an attitude of creativity. Be determined to make *your* mark. It's an important part of your pursuit of excellence.

We Can Overcome

Some of the world's greatest men and women have been saddled with disabilities and adversities but have managed to overcome them.

Cripple him, and you have a Sir Walter Scott.

Lock him in a prison cell, and you have a John Bunyan.

Bury him in the snows of Valley Forge, and you have a George Washington.

Raise him in abject poverty, and you have an Abraham Lincoln.

Subject him to bitter religious prejudice, and you have a Disraeli.

Strike him down with infantile paralysis, and he becomes a Franklin D. Roosevelt.

Burn him so severely in a schoolhouse fire that the doctors say he will never walk again, and you have a Glenn Cunningham, who set the world's record in 1934 for running a mile in 4 minutes and 6.7 seconds.

Deafen a genius composer, and you have a Ludwig van Beethoven.

Have him or her born black in a society filled with racial discrimination, and you have a Booker T. Washington, a Harriet Tubman, a Marian Anderson, a George Washington Carver, or a Martin Luther King, Jr.

Make him the first child to survive in a poor Italian family of eighteen children, and you have an Enrico Caruso.

Have him born of parents who survived a Nazi concentration camp, paralyze him from the waist down when he is four, and you have an incomparable concert violinist, Itzhak Perlman.

Call him a slow learner, "retarded," and write him off as uneducable, and you have an Albert Einstein.[3]

No road is too long for the man
who advances deliberately and
without haste; and no honors are
too distant for the man who pre-
pares himself for them with pa-
tience.

Bruyere

7

Believing in the Process

Several years ago I was browsing through the
shelves of a large Christian bookstore in Los
Angeles when a young man came up to me and
asked if he could be of assistance. For a moment I
didn't even hear his question because my eyes
were fixed on the large red button he wore on his
shirt collar. There was no slogan, no political
message—only these letters: PBPGINFWMY.

Since I've never been accused of being overly shy,
I asked him what on earth those letters meant.
And with a smile that told me he was glad I'd
asked, he said, "It means, 'Please be patient. God
is not finished with me yet.' "

What a marvelous reminder for all of us—to be

patient with ourselves and with others as we all move through this long, often tedious process called life.

Some of us learn the ropes quickly, while many of us invariably cross the stream at the widest point. But *no one at any time* has it made. No one has yet learned the answers to all the questions.

In his *Letters to His Son*, Lord Chesterfield writes, "There is hardly anybody good at everything, and there is scarcely anybody who is absolutely good for nothing."

So if your progress seems slow while it appears those around you are engaged in remarkable successes, just remember: Patience! God is not finished with you yet!

The apostle Paul recognized the importance of the Christian life as a day-by-day process when he wrote: "I do not consider myself yet to have taken hold of it. But one thing I do: Forgetting what is behind and straining toward what is ahead, I press on toward the goal to win the prize for which God has called me heavenward in Christ Jesus" (Phil. 3:13–14).

Paul was a man of particular brilliance, trained at the feet of the great Gamaliel in the traditions of ancient Israel. Through study and experience, he learned to be comfortable in both the world of the Greek and the Jew. He was an orator of no small merit and a man who would compose some of the most poignant letters—from some of the most surprising places—ever recorded in the history of humanity. This man of such great academic and spiritual accomplishment could have rested on his laurels. He could have lived as if he had arrived, but he didn't. He put aside the past, lived in the present, and pressed on toward the goal of conforming himself to the image of his Lord.

That's what it means to believe in the process. And it's an important ingredient in the pursuit of excellence.

We Americans are probably more prone to the I-want-it-now syndrome that any other people on earth. The tremendous post-World War II growth of our economy and our subsequent demand for and acquisition of endless creature comforts have somehow tricked us into believing we can have anything we want, *when we want it!*

We go on crash diets so we can lose three pounds in a day, rather than learning to eat sensibly. Our how-to-do-it books, while often helpful, too often present us with false hopes for instant riches, instant success, and instant acceptance. We often sow our wild oats and then pray for crop failure, rather than seed quality into our lives and work for a mature harvest.

All of this only demonstrates that we don't understand how things work. Lasting success, true excellence seldom comes overnight. And it always has a price.

One night after he had given one of the greatest concerts of his brilliant career, Paderewski was greeted by an overeager fan who said, "Oh, I'd give my life to be able to play like you do." Paderewski replied quietly, "I did."

If you want to be a truly effective pastor, you must work on being effective. Establish a standard for your ministry. Business people, do the same in your business. Build a reputation for excellence, and recognize that it will take time and that it will not come easily. It takes decades to grow an oak to maturity. Nature knows that it takes time to produce something that will endure.

I recall one day a dozen years ago when a young, unprepossessing seminary student came to my office to share his dream of reaching Japanese students for Christ by teaching them English in centers nearby major Japanese cities. Ken Wendling had never been to Asia, but he had the burden. I recall thinking, "Young man, it's a worthwhile idea, but what makes you think you can pull it off, with no backing, no experience, no funding?"

Today, there is possibly no ministry more significant among Japanese students than the Language Institute for Evangelism (LIFE). Ken's dream has become a reality because of his dogged determination, his never-give-up spirit. It has been a long-term process with him. Now every year teams of young people are formed for short-term service in Japan; English language centers have been established throughout the country; evangelism concerts regularly attract thousands; the Protestant church in Japan has been meaningfully supported and has evidenced growth because of the ministry of LIFE, Ken Wendling's dream and his lifetime work.

Earlier in this century, an almost-illiterate major

league baseball player, an alcoholic, came to the end of himself and one day wandered into Chicago's old Pacific Garden Mission. There he met Jesus Christ and received him as Savior and Lord. Bill Sunday's life was magnificently transformed. He immediately began to share his newly found faith with his ballplayer buddies and ultimately became the best-known evangelist in America. But—it took time. Sunday's significant ministry evolved gradually, over many years. Again, a process. Sunday overcame lack of education, the scorn of fellow preachers, suspicion of his unusual preaching style, and jealousy of peers to become a legend in his time. He became obsessed with pointing men and women and boys and girls to Christ in great evangelism crusades across America. Tens of thousands are in heaven today because of the fearless preaching and the burden of this evangelist—including my father-in-law, who met Christ in a Billy Sunday crusade. To this intrepid gospel crusader, nothing was more important than preaching Christ. He exemplified excellence in his calling to serve God through his public evangelism

It has been well said, "Those who attain to any excellence commonly spend life in some simple pursuit, for excellence is not often gained upon easier terms." Choose your top priority and stay with it.

Perhaps you're blessedly afflicted with many gifts. You're a Jack or Jane of many trades, but you really excel in none of them. Perhaps it's time to put down your shotgun and turn to your rifle. Instead of blasting recklessly into the sky of blue, hoping you'll hit something, pick your target, take careful aim, and go for the *one thing* you want most.

It's too easy to be like the Texan who waltzed up to the ticket agent at the Dallas-Fort Worth Airport and said, "Ma'am, I'd like you to sell me a first class ticket." The agent asked, "But where to, sir?" The Texan replied, "It don't really matter, ma'am. I got business everywhere."

There's nothing wrong with having business everywhere, but it's to your advantage to take care of your tasks one at a time and to recognize that each of your goals will take effort, determination, and time.

The organization I represent, World Vision, began as a dream of a young missionary-evangelist and Christian humanitarian. However, Bob Pierce never dreamed when he promised to pay for the care of one needy Chinese child, White Jade, that one day the organization he founded would care for 300,000 needy children! The ministry grew a step at a time—10 children, 100, 1,000, 10,000, 100,000. One village of hungry fed, then two, then scores. The first Pastors' Conference was sponsored overseas, soon 5 more, now over 140. One man and a secretary, no support, but a driving passion to help the needy. Thirty years later World Vision has become the largest evangelical relief and evangelism ministry in the world. This is a result of the dream of one man, of careful attention given to details, of the diligence and determination of a team of committed people, of sacrifice of time and energy—and of the blessing of God.

Excellence is a process that should occupy all our days, whether it is tied to a specific piece of work done or not. Just as you must work at life, so you must work at the spirit of excellence. It will become a part of you only through a singleness of purpose and a determination to see your goals through to the end.

Remember, "It's always too soon to quit." You and I will make mistakes today. We'll make errors in personal judgment and mistakes in administration. But we do ourselves no favors if we judge ourselves on the performance of the last several hours. Instead, we need to ask, What is our track record? What kind of progress have we made during the past six months—the past year? Are we closer to our goal? Have we gained new insights into ourselves as a result of our work?

Courage is the ability to "hang in there" five minutes longer.

We've written considerably in these chapters about attitudes, goal-setting, priorities, motivation, and believing in the long process that excellence demands. But there's another quality that's equally important: the ability to relax and enjoy.

Some time ago I came across this homily by an aging monk, Brother Jeremiah, who was reflecting on his many years of Christian service. He'd worked hard, sometimes too hard. He'd taken life seriously, often too seriously. And as he approached the end of his active service to others, he sat down and wrote these words:

> If I had my life to live over again, I'd try to make more mistakes next time. I would relax. I would limber up. I would be sillier than I have been this trip. I know of very few things I would take seriously. I would take more trips. I would climb more mountains, swim more rivers, and watch more sunsets. I would do more walking and looking. I would eat more ice cream and less beans. I would have more actual troubles and fewer imaginary ones.
>
> You see, I am one of those people who live prophylactically and sensibly and sanely, hour after hour, day after day. Oh, I've had my moments, and if I had it to do over again, I'd have more of them. In fact, I'd try to have nothing else. Just moments, one after another, instead of living so many years ahead each day. I have been one of those people who never go anywhere without a thermometer, a hot water bottle, a gargle, a raincoat, aspirin, and a parachute. If I had it to do over again, I would go places, do things, and travel lighter than I have.
>
> If I had my life to live over, I would start barefooted earlier in the spring and stay that way later in the fall. I would play more. I would ride on more merry-go-rounds. I'd pick more daisies.

In my book, *The Making of a Christian Leader*, I address the importance of such balance in our living.

> A person can become a workaholic by overcommitting himself financially, by making unrealistic plans, or simply by failing to recognize a personality

defect. Often he may use work as an escape mechanism. Thus he has to drive himself to the exclusion of what should be his priorities.

It is most unfortunate that we deplore drug and alcohol addicts but somehow promote and admire the work addict. We give him status and accept his estimate of himself. And all the while his family may be getting so little of his time and energy that they hardly know him.

Overwork is not the disease itself. It is a symptom of a deeper problem—of tension, of inadequacy, of a need to achieve—that may have neurotic implications. Unfortunately for the workaholic, he has no home; his house is only a branch office. He won't take a vacation, can't relax, dislikes weekends, can't wait for Monday, and continues to make his own load heavier by bringing more work onto himself. Such a person also is usually defending against having to get close to people.[1]

Obsessive, compulsive striving for our goals is *not* the way to pursue a life of excellence.

When the apostle John wrote his three brief but beautiful and intimate epistles, he was a very old man, possibly in his nineties. As he reflected on his life and the human needs that continued to surround him, all he chose to say, basically, was, "Little children . . . love one another."

Life has its rhythm, and the process takes many convoluted turns. The ambitions of youth are seldom the desires of the old. So much happens in the interval, and it's all part of the process.

What is happening in your interval? What are you doing to ensure that your life is holding all the splendor and promise God has intended for you? Are you devoting your energies toward a pursuit of excellence in every area of your life?

You can, and you can start today.

Now is the time to develop new habits, new goals, and new perspectives that will give your life a quality that will bring honor to the God who loved you so much that He gave His life for you.

Don't just think about it. Do it!

The poet James Russell Lowell has said it so well:

> Life is a leaf of paper white
> Whereon each one of us may write
> His word or two,
> And then comes night.
>
> Greatly begin, though thou have time
> But for a line,
> Be that sublime,
> *Not failure, but low aim, is crime.*

Notes

Chapter 1

[1]Anecdote retold from *What a Day This Can Be*, John Catoir, ed., Director of the Christophers (New York: The Christophers).

Chapter 2

[1]Og. Mandino, *The Greatest Secret in the World* (New York: Frederick Fell Pubs. Inc., 1972), p. 30.
[2]Ibid., p. 38–39.

Chapter 4

[1]Catoir, *What a Day*, p. 10.
[2]Ibid., p. 10.

Chapter 5

[1]Alfred J. Kolatch, *Guideposts* (August 1974), p. 25.

Chapter 6

[1]John Gardner, *Self Renewal* (New York: Norton, rev. ed. 1981), p. 12.
[2]From "Creative Thinking" cassette, Earl Nightengale and Whitt Schultz. Quoted in Frank Goble, *Excellence in Leadership* (Aurora, Ill.: Caroline House Pubs., 1972), p. 21.
[3]From the "anonymous" file of my friend and colleague Dr. F. Carlton Booth.

Chapter 7

[1]Ted Engstrom, *The Making of a Christian Leader* (Grand Rapids: Zondervan, 1976).